Rambles In shambles

Dani McGregor

Presentation by *BookLeaf Publishing*

Web: www.bookleafpub.com

E-mail: info@bookleafpub.com

ISBN: 9789357615792

First edition 2022

DEDICATION

Rebecca

You created everything good about me

You will endure me

You'll endure me
When my wits spray out like venom
When my spirit has fizzled
My soul only fragments held in a frail shell of
my body
You'll endure me
When I'm nothing but thistles
A guided missle
When you find your dove has a serpents tongue
You'll endure me
For without the chronic ache
How could the release be as sweet
Wretched and fickle
You'll endure me

Destiny my enemy

Survival mode, where I spend all my last lucky penny's

The space between who I imagined I would be
and who I got caught up being goes for miles
It haunts me
Now every dream, I wish away
I let them go to lighten my load

My heavy heart sunk

Heavy Season

Hey Marine, I'll be waiting at the dock for you
Hey Marine, don't lose your way
Please look for me
This season will be heavy
But I'll be waiting here forever
Until I give up my ghost
Are you lost at sea Marine? Or did you just
decide to leave

Trials of estrangement

Bred from a turncoat
& the roads you take to escape the same fate
A cowards curse, with a set of values you don't
have the skill to demonstrate
Such a wavering love
Destiny can't change its way to console every
fool
With rumination & contempt
You wouldn't even recognise me now
Untethered
You don't even recognise you

Embedded #2

The energy it takes to project my light
Blows my motor
My words are trapped behind my teeth
Mute
I was sincere, I was naive
Can you recognise me now?
Untethered

Rumination and Contempt

This place is a portal to the past
Destiny can't change her way, to console every
fool
Yet we have come to a strange future
Should we go back?

Turncoat #3 jumbled

The road taken to avoid the same fate
Somehow led me me to the bridges you you had
come to
I had my 'values'
But none of the qualities needed to enforce them
Such a wavering love

Song unsung

Blah blah blah
I don't think I've got any Poems today

What it cost to pave your path

Bitterness
A season that came late
Wistful
Took up all my time
I was always waiting for something
I'd hoped I could of forgotten by now
Bankrupted
Hijacked
Broke

A life of waiting

Crack the code and the game Is over
I'll bide my time
Eyes with the hue of the heart of a flame
Traps of indecision
FIn the freeze-frame
Moments of confusion that made up a life
Was I patient? Or did I let it slip through my
fingers?
Slip past the hands on the face of the watch
I watched and it ticked my seconds away

A revolution every hour

One revolution for every hour
Tiny enough to escape my view

I built steps to heaven but I never knew
I wasn't building them for me
I was building them for you

The blood it took to earn them and the fight to
defend what's ours

There's a revolution every hour
It's tiny
It depends what you do

Rephrase

Relinquish your duties
Sure to be taken from you in time
And I will spare you the devastation
I'll spare you wasted days
I'll spare you the growth of attachment and grant
an opportunity to pave new ways
What I used to call love I undoubtedly rephrase

Yet if our paths cross again I don't suspect you
should thank me
He who could enjoy the labour of love

These are not the days

I was the type to lift your spirit

These are not those days

I was the type to endure whether crippled or
crushed

These are not those days

If you find you cannot bare the new form I have
found

That's OK
These are not those days I could be easy to love

The aversion

The girl you loved this summer
Won't be the woman you'll love In the winter
This kind of love is fleeting
You can't anchor it any less than you can change
the turn of the seasons

If you meet the end and it all comes around
again
Don't be fool enough to try your luck

Wrung out

All that was soaked up, without conscious

Will need to be wrung out

You can't take it with you

And it gets soo heavy

What the young soak up, the tired demand to be
wrung out

Somewhere is serenity

Somewhere is serenity
Unreachable by two

Inside the mind
a lucid dream

No gate way, no stairs

But this is where I live
Inside the singuar mind with nowhere to meet
you there

Romantic indifference

A love unlike other loves
Affection scarce

A love unlike other loves
Some might say a farce

Gloomy day will have his way

A gloomy day will have his way
But the light of the moon will brighten soon
Lady Luna, the comfort of the mother